Rains & Oceans

Manisha Naskar is an introvert who grew up on books and is currently facing mid-twenty crisis. Although she is a biochemist by degree but a better description of her would be, a perpetually confused soul who finds solace in the rain, tea and ocean. Currently in Seoul, South Korea, she is pursuing PhD and ticking off items on her bucket list. To get in touch with her, drop a message on Instagram @themanishanaskar, or write her an e-mail manishanaskar081@gmail.com

PAPER PALACE PUBLISHING
web: *paperpalace.in*

This is a work of fiction. Names, characters, places and incidents are either the product of the author's imagination or are used fictitiously and any resemblance to any actual person, living or dead, events or locales is entirely coincidental.

ISBN: 978-81-940678-7-0
Price: Rs. 199

Rains & Oceans

Manisha Naskar

To the ones who have
Believed in me,
Broken me
And helped me heal.

Meet me when
The sun is at its brightest
And the day has been tiring
And we shall find rest in each other

Meet me when
Raindrops hammer our window
As we sip on tea, in each other's arms
And let laughter, calm our souls

Meet me when
The leaves say goodbye as they fall
Turning red and yellow, on to the pavement
And I'll revive in your arms

Meet me when
There is chill in the air
The branches are naked and snow drifts freely
And I'll find warmth in your hug

Meet me when
The flowers, all colorful,
Make the air heavy with their fragrance
And I'll breathe anew, in your presence

Maybe I crossed a line,
When I confessed
In the crossfire of emotions,
Friendship was dead

A crazy journey
Started with awkward greetings
Moved on to abuses
Sprinkled honesty
Shared life's anecdotes
Held each other's hands when needed
Learnt to listen, understand
Helped each other along the way
Above all, laughed like crazy
With every difficulty that we came across
Held onto each other tightly
Stumbled, fell, and got up again.

Went on crazy adventures
I tasted life
Felt happiness on my tips
Somewhere, along the way,
You fell for my smile
Love happened
Friendship took a bow
Never knew when our endless conversations
Shitty abuses and contagious laughter
Became our lifeline

Reborn

I think I lost something of me in you
The moment when I held your hand,
For the first time, watched your carefree laugh
Resonating with my giggles
Your soft gaze, lingering on my face
Watching me with tenderness
As if I was the only thing that mattered

The moment when we were
Running through the waves and I stumbled
You helped me back up
And started running again
While not letting go off of my hand

When you challenged me to hold my breath
Under the water, I refused
For I was afraid of it.
You grabbed my hand and
Pulled me underneath with you
Our heads touching, so that
I could feel your presence,
Even in absolute terror.

The moment when you grabbed my fingers
As we lay, gazing at the peaceful moon
Content with our insignificant and tiny existence
As the boat we lay on,
Drifted slowly over warm currents
Beneath the night sky

I lost a part of me in every moment
That I spent with you

I lost my worries, my frustration
And above all, my fears
And for a moment, I felt that I was free
I was happy, and I was content

And that was when I realized that
I had lost the hopeless girl I had become
I lost the frightened soul
I used to carry, deep within me
I had lost my past
My scars had faded
You had scratched my wounds
Shattered my every fragment
And had built me from the ruins
For I had lost myself
I had been replaced,
By the girl you made me to be
I was reborn from the ashes
And you were the fire that had engulfed me

The stolen kiss

Your fingers slightly caressed mine
Under the canopied sky
The moon was peeking through branches
Rest of the world was blur, passing by
You leaned in softly
Put your lips on mine
They melted against my own
I felt the stars align

You did not stop there
Pulled my soul too
Amidst all the colors in my life
I only saw blue
You tugged on my lower lip
I tasted your love
And beneath the dark sky
Having you, beside me, was enough

You

I forget my past
The wounds don't hurt
The scars seem lighter
Deeper become the words

A smile plays on my lips
The moments seem to hasten
Only when I am with you
Why does this seem to happen?

Isn't it unfair?
That the sunsets become more ethereal
With my head on your shoulder,
I tend to forget my fears

I seem calm
I laugh more
Our souls experience a magic
Touching us to the core

In your presence I seem to shine
Looks as if you don't have the faintest clue
Oh! Babe, why don't you get this?
I am happiest when I am with you

In your presence,
My soul quietly sings,
Thanks to you,
I was able to unfold my wings

Ready to take the leap,
From the highest tree
The wind beckons me babe,

It feels so free...

I might stumble badly
Or I might even fall...
Yet, I'm not worried, 'cause
I know you'll be somewhere around.

Have you fallen for me too?

The way you lean, softly
Holding my waist in your arms,
Your lips softly touch mine
And I drift away into oblivion,
The sky turns still, everything silenced
And all I want,
Is to melt right there in your arms
You become my gravity
Holding me there
And I don't want this moment to end

You hold my hand
Tugging the fingers,
Pulling me through the crowd,
Talking, smiling,
Creating memories, beautiful ones,
Tell me babe,
Aren't you afraid, even one bit?

The way you look at me
When you think I don't know
The way you smile
The way you capture me,
Beautifully, through your lens
Every moment spent with you
Seems like a dream, too good to be true.
The moments turn special
As our laughter resonates in our souls
Again, I ask, aren't you afraid,
Even one bit?

I am curious as to why
You allow me to love you so much
Aren't you afraid of the pain and hardships,
That come along with this?
I ask again, aren't you afraid
Of falling in love with me?
Or have you already?

Loving you is a choice that I made
A perfect decision of
Controlled destruction
To ruin myself piece by piece
Tear my emotions apart
And rendering myself broken

Loving you
It is something I thrive on
Even when you advise me not to
"Do not ruin yourself" you tell me
"Live your life; be strong.
You have a lot to live for."
A thousand times, you tried to warn me,
"I am an ocean,
And you don't know how to swim.
You'll drown, I might destroy you."
You begged me to stay away to even let you go
Do you even know how alluring you sound?

I fell for you unknowingly
But the choice to keep loving you
Was pure self-destruct
I chose it that way.
Your fleeting love is all I crave
It fuels me on, pulling me in
Slowly, to my own ruins...
Oh, I know how this will end
But the irony is that
I am allowing to be dragged, willingly.

It was all my fault
I realize it now
Falling in love with you
I knew I could never make you mine
Yet I gambled my heart away
I was charmed and fell for you, hard
Despite all the warnings
I went ahead and risked it all
And now, look at me
I have lost my heart
As well as you

From friends to strangers

I cannot decipher you anymore
You seem a stranger to me
An unfamiliar being, a soul I lost.
Our conversations seem forced,
To be truthful, even unnatural to some extent.
We don't have things to talk about, anymore
Your voice, devoid of the cheerfulness
It sounds irritated and tired
The fake smile you carry,
I doubt that it is fake only for me.
You seem exasperated of me, while I
Still think you are my savior.

You sound mean, you seem mean.
I am still clueless whether
It's reality or a mere façade,
To push me away from you.
And the worst part is, I can't even ask,
About this sudden change
In your temperament, in your heart.
Do I seem desperate to you?
Or a bothersome individual, like an incessant fly,
That refuses to leave you alone.

The moment I ask, you'll merely smile
And give me a stupid excuse
Or worse,
Might even ask me to hate you.
I thought you were a good human, but now,
I think you are a hollow shell, in which
My concerns resonate and your response is silence.
Tell me, am I alone on this boat, and

Is the wind blowing in the wrong direction
As I feel I am drifting away from you?

In spite of your ignorance, all I can recall
Our sweet memories
Why am I hell bent on forgiving you for the sake of them?
When the present I am in,
Is burning a hole through my chest.
It is becoming difficult to hold on and I know
That I should let go, before it burns.
But the more indifferent you become,
The stronger I want to hold on to.
It seems you have given up, a long way back
And if I do the same, I'll lose everything
I once believed in
Trust, love and above all, magic
That even sad people can have happy endings
That love is all we need in the end
And without it, life is worthless.

I don't want to give up
Even if my instinct tells me otherwise
I want to hold on, even if
It is breaking me apart and killing me;
Slowly, bit by bit,
Poisoning my memories.
I still want to hold on
To the person, in whom, I once believed in
To the person who once healed me
To the person whom I started to fall for,
Knowing that if and when I do,
He won't be there to catch me.

Us, a tragedy

Today, you broke me
Yeah, everything that was left
The broken edges,
That had begun to smoothen
The cracks that finally
Had begun to heal
The sadness that had
Started to leach out
I was trying to be whole
And above all, happy

The pretentious "hi"
Doesn't work anymore
The conversations seem
Artificial and forced
The carefreeness and liveliness
That used to engulf us...
It is missing
In its place, an empty corridor
Exists between us now
The emptiness of our words
Keep echoing there

You can never love me
Still I choose to follow my heart
In spite of the unending doom
That I was heading towards
I will still choose to live with those moments
Cherishing those few days
When I had the chance to
Have you by my side;
Smiling and loving you

Irrespective of the bitter truth
And painful separation –
That lay ahead.
But I was foolish – a foolish girl indeed
I thought friendship was above all
And let myself believe
That you were different
That you won't change
But those days have ended,
Having been reduced to beautiful memories.

The words sting now
We are so careful of what we say
You pretend to be carefree
And I, foolishly did the same.
Both of us know that
Our friendship has lost its charm
It is dead as a stone
Sinking to the bottom
Our bond is a façade,
A mere excuse
To have a conversation
To pretend that we still are
A part of each other's lives

What once we shared
It is gone and
Can never be brought back
The moments we shared,
In those, we rejoiced
I do not know whether
That'll happen ever again

Now all I can do is repent
Why did I tell you the truth?
Ignorance is bliss, I know now

The truth of this, hits me hard.
Wish I could turn back time
Loose that warmth for you
That keeps me going when you are not around
Lose everything if only
I could get our untainted friendship back

Go away
Break all bonds
Delete that number
That you are never going to call
Delete those messages
Which are now ugly reminders
Delete the photos
And those screenshots as well
For memories, unlike time
Don't dissolve slowly

Go away
Don't look back
For I am just a path
That you have already taken
I am just painful reminder,
A memory
That you'd rather forget
Travel so far
That my cries don't reach you
And my voice doesn't follow
Your shadow

Go away
Save yourself
Before the embers of my ruin
Burn you alive

Off the pedestal

I am taking you off the pedestal
Yes, it is time that I do
I have had enough of the false pretensions.
Thinking that I matter to you
Or that you even care
No more falsehoods
No more lies
It is just me who is killing myself over you
Stupid me,
Loving you with all my heart
While if I vanish from this world,
You would not even blink an eye

So, I have had enough of your indifference
For once, I have decided to trust my instinct
To ignore my heart and observe your actions
I am taking you off the pedestal
And breaking the remains
So that no one, no one
Can ever take your place again
And make me feel worthless

Voids

Ever since you left
I try to fill the space
With other people
Sometimes with their conversations
Sometimes with their little quirks
And their concern for me
I try to distract myself
From the fact that you are gone
And that I don't care
But I fail. Oh babe, I fail.
Every time

I try to find people
Who can substitute your presence
It took me a lot of time to realize that
The void you left
Is like a missing space in jigsaw puzzle.
However much I may try
No one else will ever fit
The way you did.

Imprisoned

I look back at the old photographs and smile
Wishing, I could go back in time
And relive those days
Past leaves us with memories
And that I think, is the saddest part
For they remind me,
What once was,
And what won't be ever again.

I miss your eyes on me
Your slightly crooked nose
The curve of your lips
The wound on your chin
The way you call me
When I am looking somewhere else
The way you lay your head on my shoulders
And ramble about your life
The way you doze off there,
Looking so peaceful, that,
For a moment, my heart skipped a beat
The way you look at me,
When I am looking at you, through the lens
The way you argue with me
Even though I am usually right
I miss everything babe, everything
And now, reliving the memories
Made me realize what we had
And how it would be never brought back

Ironically, there lies the beauty of it
Something so pure and magical that
It cannot be destroyed by our present.

Those moments of madness and absolute joy
Those days of pure innocence
Maybe they don't matter to you much
But I know their real worth
For I had tasted my freedom for the first time
Only to be imprisoned by feelings for you

I will burn your promises
On the pyre of regret
So that nothing is left of the
Hollow vows that you promised

The remains of our conversation
Shall be buried deep in soil
For your words are what
I fell in love with

Survive

I have been told by someone
That when people leave
They take a part of you, with themselves
So, tell me,
What did you take?
My laughter
That you said reflected my soul...
Or you chose to take my calmness
Because what remains is
Unrelenting restlessness

I wish you had taken my memories
Of both joy and sorrow
Or my thoughts of you
So that when you left,
These wild pangs of pain
Wouldn't have torn me apart.

Are you happy with whatever you took?
And what about me?
Limping through the pain,
Crying and wondering
Whether the hole you created in my heart
Will ever heal

Will telling you that I am missing you
Make any difference?
Perhaps not!
That's why I prefer to delete those texts I sometimes write
To soothe myself into believing
That I do not miss you.
And when the memories come

I sob and fall asleep
Will there be a morning,
When I don't have to wake up, missing you?

I am trying to outlive the pain
That you've given me
Ever since the day you left
I have become a pretense
A girl,
Pretending to love life
A girl, hoping to live life as per her choices
A girl pretending to think that
Whatever happens, happens for the best

I am trying to survive
Through some quotes and lines
Written from the experience of others
Trying to outrun your memories
Trying to breathe through the broken ribs and cracked skin
Through the parched lips and tears
Through every good thing that ever happened to us
Trying to live
Trying to breathe

Courage

You are afraid
You are scared
Frightened that
What happened before
Will happen again
Your past haunts you.
You don't want to commit
The same mistake again;
So whenever love knocks on your door,
You run, run away
As far as you can

All I ask is how long
Will you keep doing that?
Unfortunately, I love you
And will continue to do so
Irrespective of what logic says
And although I am afraid
You will run away
Maybe too far, for too long
But somewhere, deep down
I know that, you love me enough,
To come back,
Always

Time turns back

You came back
When all hope had been demolished.
You turned back
Maybe for love
Maybe for me,
But you did
And it makes me wonder why?

You say that we come with an end date
Our roads diverge somewhere
And you will be with me
For as long as possible for you to be.
Like a child, I believe in you
And enjoy this momentary happiness that you bring

Why am I willing to love you so much?
Why am I ready to torture myself every day, for your sake?
When sanity clearly states that
I should not fall for you again
I should not give you another chance
I should erase you from my heart,
Why am I craving your presence
Your momentary existence
And allowing you back in my life
Allowing me to rely on you even more deeply and
Making the mistake everyone would avoid

I guess this is what people call love
When you love the person wholly,
All you care about is the present
And how happy does that person make you?
I am choosing you

For now, for today
And when tomorrow comes with its grim realities
I will fight for you
Again.

Anomaly

I am fooling myself into believing that
Whatever we have is bliss
I am clutching at you
To breathe, to exist
Knowing full well that it's not worth it

You will go and won't even look back
I am hoping against hope
Or rather building expectations
Like a house of cards
That will shatter at the slightest nudge of truth
You are not mine
And never will be
Knowing that, why am I adamant
In struggling to hold on to you,
Like holding water in my hands.

Some things are not meant to be
And our spark of love, the transient bond of ours
Is just another anomaly

It takes a lot of courage to move.
To stand up, collect the broken pieces, and keep walking
To never look back
And remember how beautiful it had been?
To not regret, what could have been
True, it takes a lot of strength,
To make peace with the past and forget

But I feel it takes even more strength
To not give up
To risk it all
To burn yourself till the end
To make sure that there are no regrets left
To make sure that there is no stone left unturned
It takes a lot of strength to
Keep yourself alive everyday
And live through the pain again and again

Trail of destruction

I knock endlessly, at your door
With a hope that you'd reply
With a hope that you'd turn back.

How beautifully you have shattered me.
But you refuse to turn back
Refuse to even glance once at me
Makes me wonder, what we had
What was it for you?
Did I matter?

How could you shun me so easily?
Cast me aside, as if I did not matter
And the worst part is,
Even though this had happened before,
I did not learn my lesson

How do you find the strength,
The determination to
Go back on every word
That erupted from your lips
Going back on every promise
Hurting the one person who matters
Shattering their belief in love

Don't you think it is a bit selfish
A bit, just a tiny bit
That, to build yourself, to grow
You destroy the very person
Who supported you and cared for you, all along?

Don't you owe them something?
An apology or an explanation?

Or may be some left-over love
Because, people like me,
They keep going back through those conversations
Again and again
Looking for signs of crumble
Wondering where it went wrong
What was the mistake?
And thus, lose their sanity

Loving your indifference

I know what you are doing
Ignoring me like I do not exist
Pretending to not care anymore
And diminishing me to almost nothingness
I know babe, I know the trick
Pushing people away
When you are about to get attached
Putting your armour up again
Against emotions, against love
Because you cannot go through the torture
One more time

You warn me of the consequences
You ask me to stay away
No more feelings,
What was there, has evaporated
Always, asking me not to
Fall irrevocably for you

I know how vulnerable you are
How far you have come
You are wiser now,
And don't want to go down that path
Again, ever again

I will just keep you loving then
While you erase your existence from my life
I will be there
Daring to love you through your indifferences
Daring to hold your hand
To show you what love feels like.
Once more.

Trying to love someone else
Instead of you
That, would be cheating my heart
Asking you to love me back,
Well, it won't be fair to you?
Would it?

Letting go of people

I am learning slowly
Letting go of people
Their words, their habits, their love
We are made by the people that we meet
We imbibe their characters,
We cherish their memories
Making them, a part of us

I am eliminating those pieces of myself
Making myself whole again
I want to fall out of love now
This pain, of loving you,
Is getting unbearable?
The pain kicks you into a corner
And leaves you shattered
And how do you deal with something
That is solely a matter of the mind?
The eyes don't dry
Neither does the heart
Drowned by the emotions and feelings
You choke.
This unrequited love
Slowly kill you, bit by bit
Falling in love was a beautiful thing
For us, it was short lived,
Now I just want to fall out of it,

More than you,
It's your memories that are killing me

Forgive yourself
For loving them too much
For making them your priority
For patiently waiting for them
Whenever they ignored you
Or made you feel less
Than your worth.

Forgive yourself
For hurting yourself
Over and over again
Over the same pieces of a broken heart
As you never learnt your own worth

Forgive yourself
For everything you tried that did not workout
For taking more time to heal
For trusting someone too much
For not being able to move on, easily

Before you gather the courage to stand up again,
Forgive

Goodbye

I am a coward
Not among the brave ones out there
Who are master of their heart
As well as their emotions.
I am a feeble soul
Who dwells in her mind a lot
And believes that like fairytales,
Life also comes with happy endings

And I have made my peace with that
I cannot make you love me
I cannot make you stay
If you wanted to do that
You wouldn't have left.
I let my worth be determined by your presence
Whether you chose to love me or not
Whether you chose to hear your heart and love me back
Whether you chose to stay
I have given up the expectations
I am holding on to the love
But not to you
I have made peace with the fact that
As much as I can love you
I can never ever make you love me.
Unrequited love is the worst
Neither can I make my heart forget you
Nor can I force you to love me

So, I am letting you go.
I will love you
And eventually with time,
Gather enough strength to accept that

We were not meant to be
Maybe then, I will somehow, find a closure.
No anger, no regrets
Just a sense of sadness of what we could have been

I will gather courage
Smile and be brave
And try to live through each day
Surviving the onslaught of your memories
Slowly, until the day
When your name doesn't hurt anymore
Or reminiscing our memories
Isn't something that I avoid
I will try to love you
Till I don't anymore.

Also Read

NINE LIVES. THREE STORIES. ONE BOOK.
'A book with zero negative reviews till date!'
ONCE UPON a TIME
'A brutally honest saga of love, dreams and real life.'
SAURAV CHHAWCHHARIA

#ZeroNegativeReviews

"A perfect blend of romance, fiction and thrill. The plot twists and cliffhangers will make sure you finish the book in one sitting. I just can't keep away from it. This is a book you should read if you're a reader and definitely read if you're a writer."

– Dhwani Parmar

"The way the life of Samir, Rashid and slums is depicted. And that sweet love story which death overtook even before it started: clearly signifies how your potential can be wasted unknowingly, on the other hand how someone low can emerge out! Man, I want a sequel to this!"

– Kushal Raut

"As John Green said and here I quote: *Sometimes, you read a book and it fills you with this weird evangelical zeal, and you become convinced that the shattered world will never be put together unless and until all living humans read the book!* Once Upon A Time is that book. And though I want to smite you for breaking my heart again and again, I can't help but say that I'm thankful that you wrote this and you did a pretty good job in ripping my heart out but thanks anyway!"

– Anjali Dedha

Message **@iamsauravc** on Instagram to buy!

www.ingramcontent.com/pod-product-compliance
Lightning Source LLC
LaVergne TN
LVHW041441170726
843492LV00008B/2745